Your Friends Are Waiting

The Very Simple, Easy Guide to Joining Facebook

Amber Grove

DEDICATION

This is to my Mom and Dad and all the other Baby Boomers out there, who just want a simple guide to joining Facebook. It's never too late to get connected!

CONTENTS

ACKNOWLEDGMENTS

Thanks Mom. This is for you. If it wasn't for all your questions, I wouldn't write all these guides! Oh, and to Facebook, since you're the ones who started this craziness!

1 - GETTING STARTED

You don't have to know anything about computers to be on Facebook.

You don't even have to have any friends to be on Facebook.

But you soon will.

This is a very simple and basic guide on how to join Facebook. And although the last statistics I saw said that there are over 500 million users, and counting (apparently 1 million users sign up per week), I still know a lot of people who have not taken the Facebook plunge. My parents and in-laws being a few of them. So Mom, this is for you! And all the other parents, grandparents, and friends out there, who just aren't sure where to start.

And don't worry. You haven't missed much – except maybe what a few hundred of your "friends" have been doing for the past couple years….

2 - SIGNING UP

Feeling out of the loop? Not sure where to start? Don't worry, this easy guide will help take the "mystery" out of Facebook.

Email Address

First of all, <u>get an email address</u>, if you don't already have one. *(If you don't have an email, please see appendix A at the end of this guide on the how to set up a gmail [google email] account.)* I would strongly recommend not using a work email for Facebook, unless you plan on setting up your Facebook account for work purposes.

Now that you have determined which email address you are going to use, <u>go to the internet</u> and <u>type</u> in <u>www.facebook.com</u>.The first screen you see will look like this:

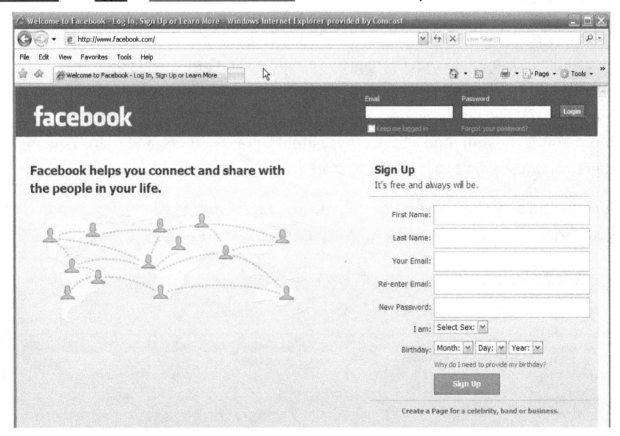

Fill out the Sign Up area, as seen below:

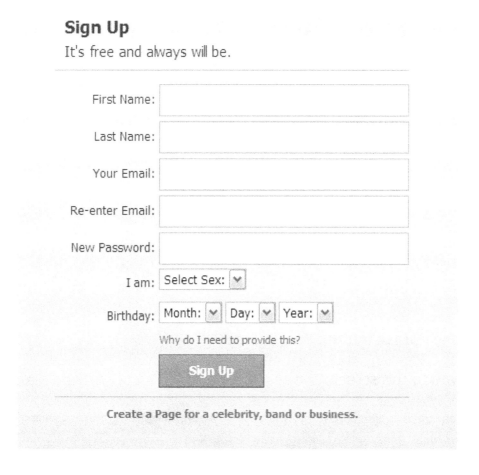

For example, if your name is Bobbie Babyboomer. You <u>enter</u> your name, email, password, sex and birthdate. Make sure you enter a valid email address, as this email will be used by Facebook to notify you of messages and friend requests.

After you've filled out the information, press **<u>SIGN UP!</u>**

This will bring you to this screen:

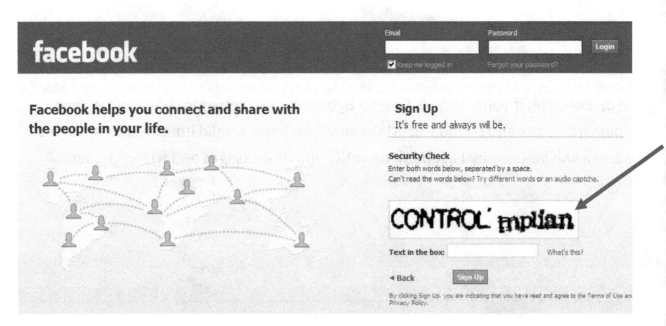

It may be hard to read, but you must <u>type</u> in the words you see. This is to make sure you are a live human being. If it's too hard to read, <u>click</u> on "try different words". Or, if you have speakers, <u>click</u> on *"audio captcha"*, and type the words they say. Don't worry if you mess up, they will give you another chance.

*Here is also where they have Terms of Use and Privacy Policy. It's not a bad idea to read it, as you are agreeing to these terms by signing up. However, if you don't agree, you don't get to be on Facebook, so I guess millions of users have decided that they are ok with these terms and policies. And of course, like most, it's a whole lot of legal mumble jumble that most of us are too busy or too lazy to read, or we wouldn't understand it anyway.

3 - ALL ABOUT YOU

Onto the next screen. Which is, All About **YOU!**

Step 1 – Find Friends

It's basically asking you if you want Facebook to use your email to connect you to your list of friends. You could do this, but I would go back to it later. Let's just get you all signed up first. <u>Click</u> on "Skip this Step".

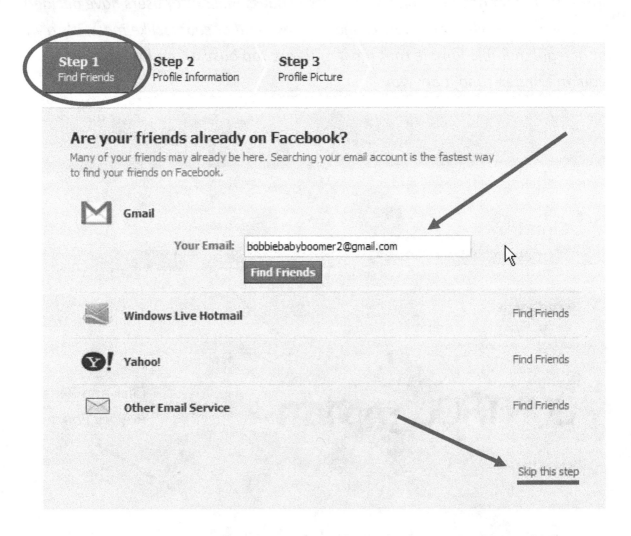

Step 2 – Profile Information

Start with the basics.   Only <u>type</u> in the information you would like to share.
Facebook uses this information to suggest people that you may want to be
Facebook friends with, or to connect you to people that you already know based on
your profile information. For example, if you went to Jefferson High School,
Facebook may use this information to help you find other people who went to
Jefferson High School. This is the same with Colleges/Universities and Employers.
You can skip this information, if you don't want to fill it in right now. You can
always add it later. Otherwise, fill in the information and <u>click</u> on **Save & Continue.**

Step 3 – Profile Picture

This is where you get to show the World (well, at least 1/12 of the World) how great you look! Or, if you prefer, you can show a picture of your child, grandchild, dog, cat, horse, chicken, or who knows what! You can use any random picture, as long as it yours, and as long as it's not of someone else. But most people really do prefer to see you, at least at first.

You can upload (add) your photo by <u>clicking</u> "Upload a Photo" and then browse (search) your computer files to find the photo you want to use, <u>double-click</u> on your picture and **Presto**! You are a Face on Facebook!

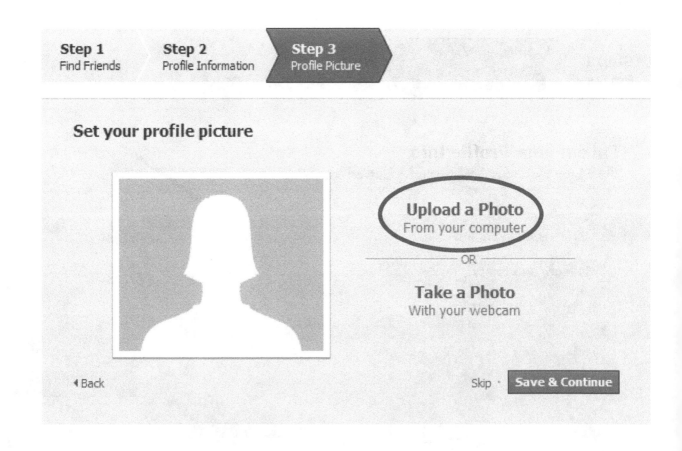

Double-Click on a photo from your computer folder

Click on Save & Continue.

Again, you can skip this step if you'd like to add a picture later.

4 - WELCOME TO FACEBOOK

Welcome to FACEBOOK!

You must now complete the sign-up process.

GO TO YOUR EMAIL

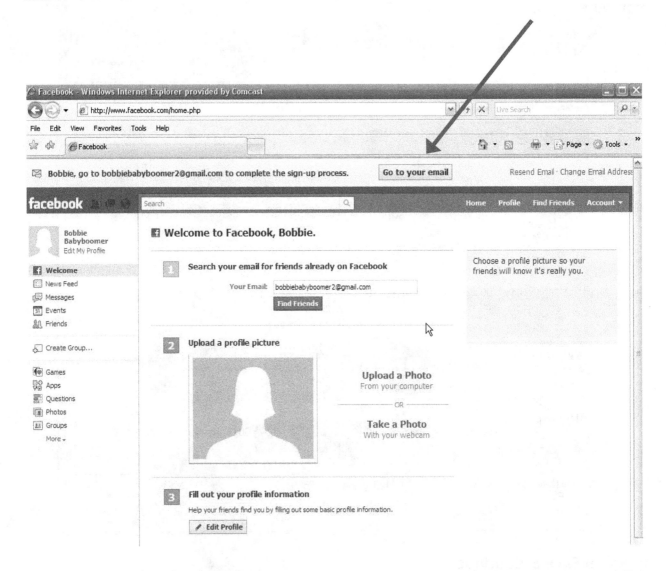

You will have a message from Facebook.

<u>Click</u> and <u>Open</u> the message.

This is to verify your email address and complete the sign-up process.

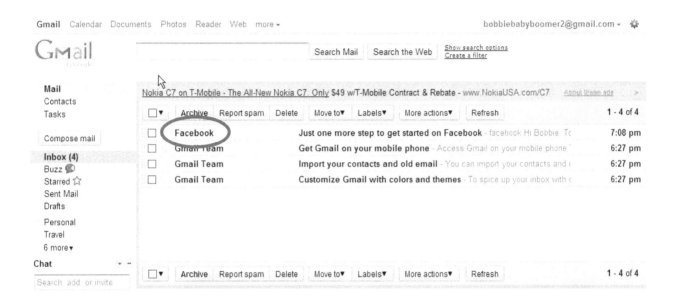

<u>Click</u> on **COMPLETE SIGN-UP**

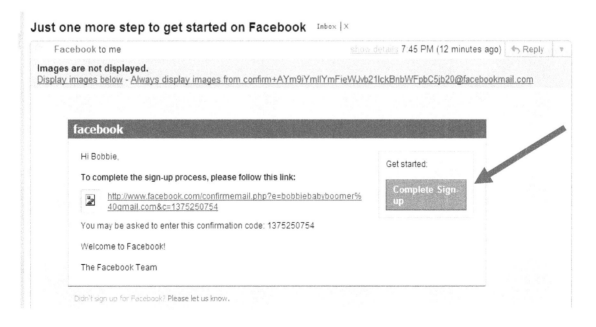

TaDa! You are now on Facebook!

Welcome!

☐ Welcome to Facebook, Bobbie.

---

1 **Search your email for friends already on Facebook**

Your Email: [   ]

Email Password: [   ]

Find Friends

🔒 Facebook won't store your password.

---

2 **Upload a profile picture**

Upload a Photo
From your computer

— OR —

Take a Photo
With your webcam

---

3 **Fill out your profile information**

Help your friends find you by filling out some basic profile information.

✏ **Edit Profile**

---

5 - NOW WHAT?

You have now joined over 125 million Americans and over 375 million people around the world on Facebook.

NOW WHAT???

The next screen brings you to a basic overview of what you've done so far.

1 – You can FIND FRIENDS

2 – Upload a Profile Picture

3 – Fill out your Profile Information

Moving on, the next step is:

4 – Activate your Phone.

Activating your phone is the next step. You can decide if you want to get your Facebook notifications via your mobile phone. If you want this ability, you might want to add this later, as often times when you first join Facebook you receive a lot of messages. Everyone is just so happy you've decided to join!

 Activate your mobile phone

- Receive texts with your friends' Status Updates and Messages instantly.
- Update your Status and Message friends using SMS.

Register for Facebook Text Messages

Already received a confirmation code?

5 – Find People you know

This is a great way to start. You can start searching for people immediately. However, I, personally wouldn't do this until you do number 6. I think Number 6 is the most important step. (I'm just looking out for you, Mom!).

6 – Control What Information You Share

I'm not the paranoid type. But I did grow up with a lawyer as a father, so I do error on the cautious side. I like to keep what the world sees about me to a minimal. This is where you decide who gets to see the information that you post on your profile. You can also decide who gets to even see your profile. Which is great. Quite frankly, I really don't need to connect to EVERYONE from my past. I'm sure there's probably a reason why I haven't talked to some people in 20 years. Just sayin…

Anyway, on to my next point. You can read stories, upon stories, of Facebook connections. Some good, some not so good. But luckily, you can really control a lot of the information you share on Facebook. And this is where you make some of these decisions.

5 Find people you know

Search by name or look for classmates and coworkers.

Enter a name or email 🔍

6 Control what information you share

Learn more about privacy on Facebook.

6 - TO SHARE OR NOT TO SHARE

To Share or not to Share?

That is the question.

Controlling How You Share

Facebook is about sharing. Our privacy controls give you the power to decide what and how much you share. Learn how to manage who can see your information on and off Facebook. See what's new

Read our privacy policy · Learn about privacy and ads

Privacy Controls   Edit your privacy settings

The settings you choose control which people and apps can see your information. You can share your information with friends, friends of friends or everyone, and we offer presets to help you do that. Or, if you prefer, you can customize your settings.

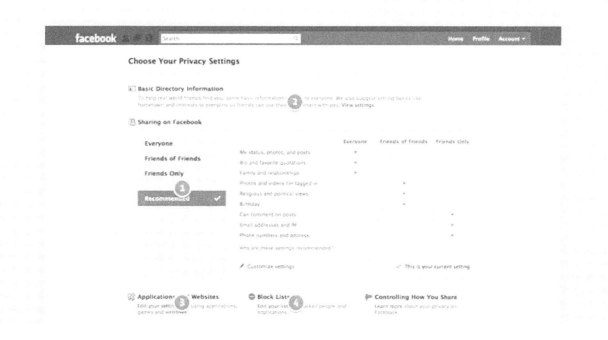

There are 4 main sections to controlling your privacy settings.

1 - Sharing on Facebook (who sees what)

2 - Basic Directory Settings – Initial info (who sees your profile info)

3 – Applications (mobile applications, etc)

4 - Block Lists – Even after you control your settings, you can still block certain people from seeing your profile.

I don't need to go step by step through each one of these, as that could make this guide become a really large book. However, I will show you the basics, so you are aware and can make informed decisions.

Anytime you want to change your privacy settings, go to:

Account – Privacy Settings

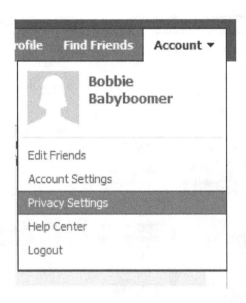

1 – Sharing on Facebook

The default looks like this. You can view the default settings, by <u>clicking</u> **"view settings"** or you can customize it, by <u>clicking</u> on the **"customize settings"** link. (Which, of course, I did. I like a little more privacy. But the recommendations of Facebook are ok, as well.)

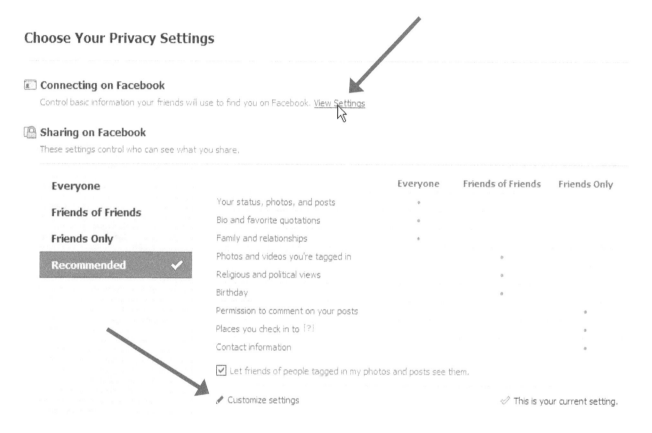

Based on your profile and information you want to share on Facebook, you choose whether you want to share this information with:
- **Everyone**
- **Friends of Friends**
- **Friends Only**

To view or change these settings – go to <u>View Settings</u>.

2 – View Settings / Basic Directory Settings

For the most part, this looks good to me. You basically choose from the drop-down menu who you want to see your profile info – Everyone, Friends of Friends, or just Friends. Review for yourself and decide how much you want others to see of you.

Once you have updated your settings, **click** on "Back to Privacy."

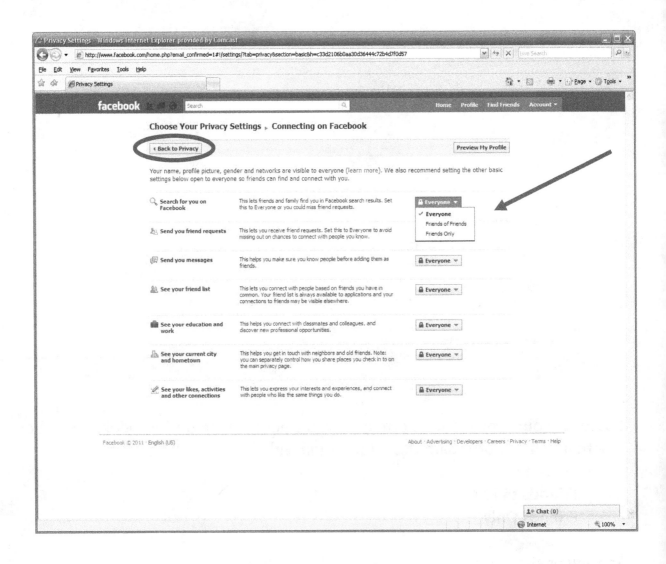

Customize Settings

To customize your privacy settings, and really narrow down who gets to see what information you share, **go** to "Customize Settings" and choose who you will allow to see what you post. I would strongly recommend really thinking about what you post and who gets to see what you post. Do you really want some of your friends' friends seeing what you post? Are all your friends, really friends?

Make sure you check **"Things Others Share"** as well. Remember, people share a lot of information on Facebook. And even though *YOU* may have just joined Facebook, a picture of you could have already been posted on someone else's Facebook page.

Choose Your Privacy Settings ▸ Customize settings

| ◂ Back to Privacy | Preview My Profile |

Customize who can see and comment on things you share, things on your Wall and things you're tagged in.

Things I share

Posts by me
Default setting for posts, including status updates and photos
🔒 Everyone ▾
  ✓ **Everyone**
  Friends of Friends
  Friends Only
  Customize

Family

Relationships

Interested in
🔒 Everyone ▾

Bio and favorite quotations
🔒 Everyone ▾

Website
🔒 Everyone ▾

Religious and political views
🔒 Friends of Friends ▾

Birthday
🔒 Friends of Friends ▾

Places you check in to
🔒 Friends Only ▾

Include me in "People Here Now" after I check in
Visible to friends and people checked in nearby (See an example)
☑ Enable

Edit privacy settings for existing photo albums and videos.

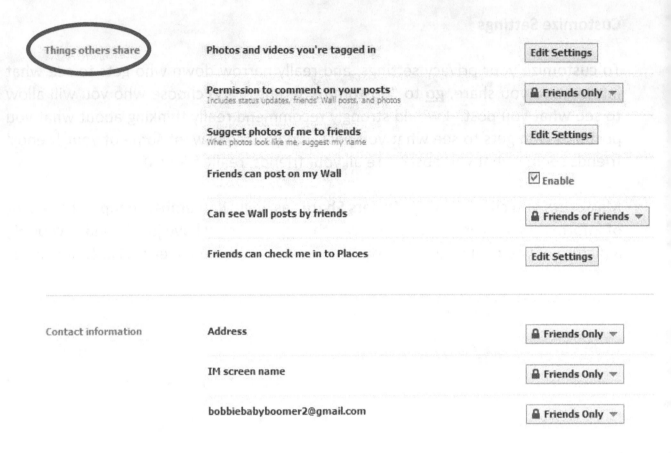

3 – Apps and Websites

This controls your privacy settings for other applications, games and websites. If you are going to use these applications, take a look at this. Take special note of "public search". This is a very important setting where you decide if someone makes a public search for you, using any type of search engine, if you are ok with them showing a preview of your Facebook profile. This, of course, is up to you. Interestingly enough, my alma mater found me this way. I'm now "donating" to the alumni association. If only I'd changed this setting earlier!

Apps and Websites
Edit your settings for using apps, games and websites.

Block Lists
Edit your lists of blocked people and apps.

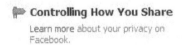

Controlling How You Share
Learn more about your privacy on Facebook.

Choose Your Privacy Settings ▶ Apps, Games and Websites

◀ Back to Privacy

On Facebook, your name, profile picture, gender and networks are visible to everyone (Learn Why). Also, by default, apps have access to your friends list and any information you choose to share with everyone.

You can change what you share with apps using these settings:

Apps you use	You're not currently using any apps, games or websites. Visit the apps dashboard or games dashboard to get started. ✎ Turn off all platform apps.	Edit Settings
Info accessible through your friends	Control what information is available to apps and websites when your friends use them.	Edit Settings
Game and app activity	Who can see your recent games and app activity.	🔒 Friends Only ▾
Instant personalization	Lets you see relevant information about your friends the moment you arrive on select partner websites.	Edit Settings
Public search	Show a preview of your Facebook profile when people look for you using a search engine.	Edit Settings

Now, click "Back to Privacy."

4 – Block Lists

Yep. This is a good one. If you don't want a particular person to find you, enter their name here. No guarantees, but it helps.

Choose Your Privacy Settings ▸ Block Lists

◂ Back to Privacy

| Block users | Once you block someone, that person can no longer be your friend on Facebook or interact with you (except within applications and games you both use). |

Name: [   ] **Block This User**

Email: [   ] **Block This User**

You haven't added anyone to your block list.

Block app invites — Once you block app invites from someone, you'll automatically ignore future app requests from that friend. To block invites from a specific friend, click the "Ignore All Invites From This Friend" link under your latest request.

Block invites from: [Type the name of a friend...]

You haven't blocked invites from anyone.

Block event invites — Once you block event invites from someone, you'll automatically ignore future event requests from that friend.

Block invites from: [Type the name of a friend...]

You haven't blocked event invites from anyone.

Click "Back to Privacy."

5 - Controlling How You Share

There's a great deal of information on privacy controls, sharing, connecting, ads, minors on Facebook and more on the **"Controlling How You Share"** area. I would strongly recommend anyone who signs up for Facebook read this information.

7 - AH, PRIVACY

As you can imagine, nothing you actually say or post on Facebook is actually private. You are posting whatever you say to the world wide web. And, of course, people at Facebook have ALL the information you post. Which is why the founders of Facebook are sitting on billions of dollars. They have demographic and marketing information that companies around the world can only dream of possessing. Not approximate information on people – but **exact** information on currently around 1/12 of the world. Who they are, how old they are, educational background, relationship status, likes, dislikes, etc. And they didn't even have to pay for it. We, by choice, gave them this information. Brilliant, I must say.

But regardless of the information that we voluntarily *give* Facebook, we do control how much information other Facebook users get to see. I think this is the most important part of this guide to joining Facebook. But then, again, I error a little on the cautious side. One thing I've learned by living with a lawyer is: anything in writing can come back to haunt you. So, depending on who you are, what you do, and what you've done, may determine your settings. Remember, it's not just *your friends* on Facebook. People use it to find their long lost father, mother, daughter, or son. Or detectives and police use it to back-up their cases or find out what "criminals" or "could be criminals" are doing. Exes use it against their ex-spouses or against the father/mother of their children. Colleges and employers use it to look up applicants… And the list goes on and on.

8 - HOW DO I LOOK?

Ok. Back to Facebook and your profile!

Congratulations! Your profile is complete. You may want to review it, or add more information at this time. But you are now ready to become a part of:

THE WORLD OF FACEBOOK!

Or as others may say **"The Facebook Obsession "**.

So, ready to see *YOUR* Face of Facebook!? <u>Click</u> on "Profile" and there you are!

9 - JOINING THE MOVEMENT

From here, you are pretty much on your own. I'd suggest searching for a couple of your friends that you know are on Facebook, using the search feature, or go to "friends" on the left of your screen. From there, you'll get many more friend suggestions, and it will keep going from there. Or you can search using your email.

You can be as active or inactive as you'd like to be. My husband signed up, and he received 75 friend requests in the first week! I've been on it awhile, and have a couple hundred friends, but I now probably only get a new request once a week.

10 - REQUESTING/ACCEPTING A FRIEND

Once you "find a friend" <u>click</u> on **"Add as Friend"**. A request will be sent to him/her and he/she will choose whether or not to accept you as his/her friend. The same goes the other direction, others will send you a friendship request, and you can choose whether or not to become their friend. This is where it can get tricky. Do you want your mom to be a friend? Do you want your child or grandchild to be your friend? What about your boss? Or Co-Worker? Only you can decide....

Searching for Friends

Requesting to be a Friend

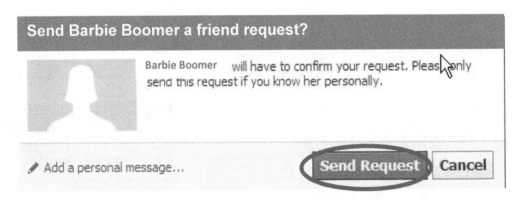

Confirming Friends

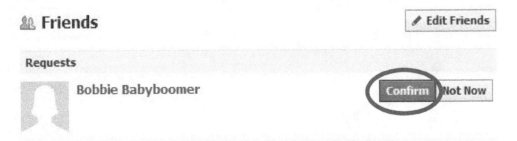

Just searching for your friends randomly, can be very daunting. It's amazing how many people in this world have the same name! So using Facebook to search for you, can definitely be helpful. Or have your friends who are already on Facebook send you a request, to get you started.

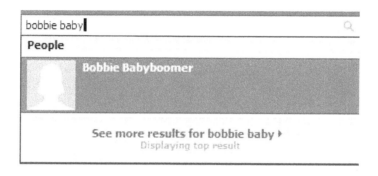

11 - WHAT DID YOU HAVE FOR DINNER?

You are now on Facebook and have lots of friends. Lucky YOU! You now get to hear what everyone is doing in their life! And, of course, you get to share what you are doing as well! This can be an excellent place to update people on your life - vacations, events, kids/grandkids/dog, etc. Just post your comments on:

THE NEWSFEED

For everyone to see!

Just click on **"News Feed"** to get started!

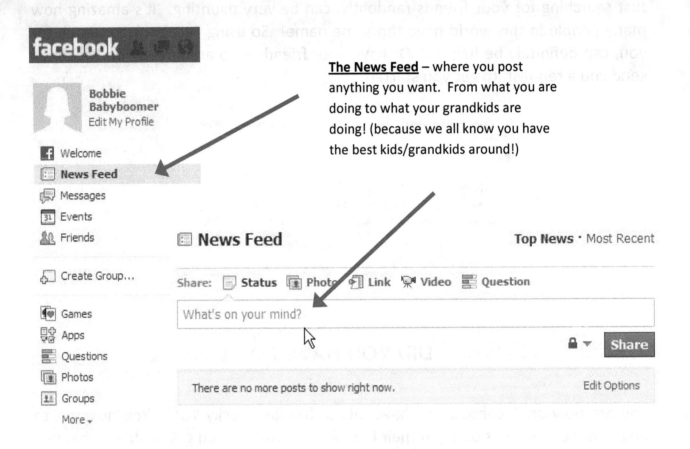

The News Feed – where you post anything you want. From what you are doing to what your grandkids are doing! (because we all know you have the best kids/grandkids around!)

And, of course, you can also see what all your friends are doing. And what their kids/grandkids are doing, and their dog... or whatever else is on people's minds. And somehow, some of them are suddenly entertaining, even downright funny. But seriously, most people don't care what you are having for dinner – unless, of course, you plan on sharing the recipe! (Don't worry, if you don't get it now, you will....)

YOUR FRIENDS ARE WAITING

12 - ALL THE OTHER STUFF

That's the basics. Of course, there's a lot more you can do on FACEBOOK, if you want to – games, applications, post photos/videos, notes, links and even more if you want to use it for business purposes. But that's for another guide. So for now,

Congratulations!

You are now part of the Facebook phenomenon. Whether that's a good or a bad thing, that's for you to decide. I've been on it for years, and I still don't know!

But good luck and have fun finding and making friends!

GLOSSARY

Tagged – to be named in a picture

Like – self-explanatory, people clicking the like button to mean they "like" something

Like (a business) – You like a certain business or organization, then you will get updates on them

Friend – anyone you agreed to be your "friend" and allow them to see your info

Friend of a Friend – you may not know them, but one of your friends does. They have access to as much info as you give them

BeFriend – to decide to be friends with someone

DeFriend – to decide to not be friends with someone anymore

APPENDIX A – SETTING UP AN EMAIL

There are many different types of free email accounts on the web. Take your pick – yahoo, gmail, etc. My favorite is gmail, so here are the simple steps to setting up a gmail (email) account.

Type in www.google.com.

Click on **GMAIL**

Click on **CREATE AN ACCOUNT**

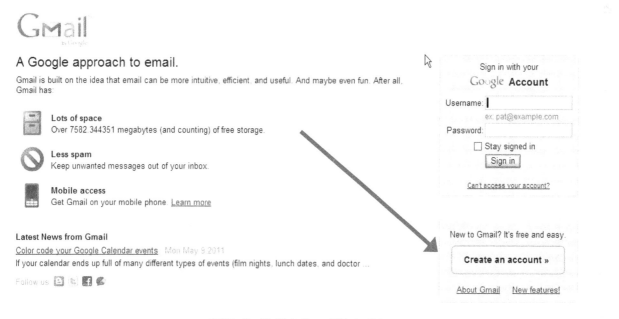

Getting Started with GMAIL

Here is where you put the basic information about you for your email account. You add your **first and last name** (this is what people will see) and then choose what you want your **email name** to be. The key here is you have to **"check availability"** to make sure someone else doesn't already have this email address. If this name has already been taken, google will give you some suggestions, or you can try another name. Keep trying this until you find one that you like and hasn't been used by someone else. Remember, this is the email address that you will use for Facebook and other things, so it should represent you in some way.

Create an Account

Your Google Account gives you access to Gmail and other Google services. If you already have a Google Account, can sign in here.

Get started with Gmail

First name:	Bobbie
Last name:	Babyboomer
Desired Login Name:	BobbieBabyBoomer2

@gmail.com

Examples: JSmith, John.Smith

    check availability!

Choose a password:

Minimum of 8 characters in length.

Re-enter password:

☐ Stay signed in

☑ Enable Web History Learn More

Default Homepage ☑ Set Google as my default homepage.
Your default homepage in your browser is the first page that appears when you open your browser.

Security question: Choose a question ...
If you forget your password we will ask for the answer to your security question. Learn More

Answer:

Recovery email:
This address is used to authenticate your account should you ever encounter problems or forget your password. If you do not have another email address, you may leave this field blank. Learn More

Password strength:

Next **choose a password**. Make sure it's something you won't forget, but that's it not too easy for others to figure out. It's always good to add a number to your password, such as ***alaska555***.

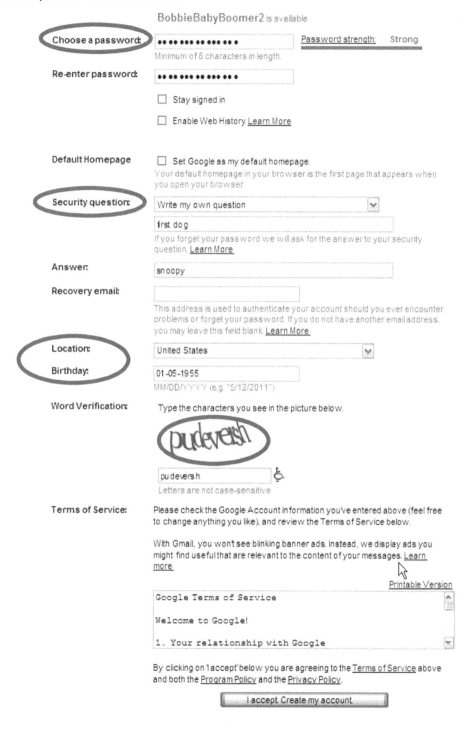

I would **NOT** choose, **"stay signed in",** or **"enable web history"** but you could use "google" as your default homepage, if you are using *YOUR* computer.

Next, choose a **security question (and answer),** in case you forget your password. This is the only way to get back on your email, if you forget your password sometime in the future. You can also add a recovery email, if you have another email address, or you can use a trusted relative/friends email for this information.

Next, enter your location and birthday.

Lastly, you must enter the words you see for **word verification** (to make sure you are a human being). Don't worry, if you get it wrong, because it's hard to see, they will give you another try. Click on **"I accept Create my account"**

That's it. You now have a gmail account! Now you can use this for Facebook, or give it to other people to send you emails.

Your email is your login name@gmail.com
For example, my email is bobbybabyboomer@gmail.com

To see your email, go to **"Show me my account"**

Later, you will go here to finish signing up for Facebook.

ABOUT THE AUTHOR

Amber Grove is a "thirty-something" mom and business woman. But her very important side job is helping all her relatives catch up on technology!

Disclaimer

This is just a guide. The author is not liable for any decisions made regarding how to join Facebook or any other choices, results or outcomes made in regards to joining Facebook. The author is also not responsible for this guides accuracy, as we all know technology changes by the minute, sometimes, by the second. Seriously, who can keep up???